Gymnastics

Rebecca Hunter

Photography by Chris Fairclough

W
FRANKLIN WATTS
LONDON • SYDNEY

First published in 2008 by
Franklin Watts
338 Euston Road
London NW1 3BH

Franklin Watts Australia
Level 17/207 Kent Street
Sydney, NSW 2000

ISBN: 978 0 7496 7834 0

Dewey classification number: 796.44

A CIP catalogue record for this book is available
from the British Library.

Planning and production by Discovery Books Limited
Editor: Rebecca Hunter
Designer: Ian Winton
Photography: Chris Fairclough
Consultant: Helene Cook, BSc Hons Coaching Science, GGL4, WAL3
and BG Tutor & Examiner

The author, packager and publisher would like to thank the following
people for their participation in this book: Helene Cook, Samantha Morris
and the gymnasts of Border Counties School of Gymnastics, Oswestry.

Printed in China

Franklin Watts is a division of Hachette Children's Books,
an Hachette Livre UK company
www.hachettelivre.co.uk

Contents

Gymnastics

Gymnastics is a sport that first started over 2,000 years ago in ancient Greece. It involves positions and movements, so gymnasts need to have good strength, **flexibility** and balance.

Equipment

Gymnasts use many different pieces of **apparatus**. Warming-up exercises and many floor skills are done on large, soft mats for comfort and safety.

Kit

Gymnasts must wear clothing that doesn't restrict their movement. It must be made of lightweight and stretchy material. Girls wear **leotards** and boys wear leotards with shorts, or shorts and a vest top.

Tracksuits can be worn over the basic kit to keep you warm before performing. Gymnastics is usually performed in bare feet. Hair should be tied back and jewellery removed.

Warning!

Doing gymnastics is both fun and energetic but it can also be dangerous. Do not attempt to get into positions or try moves until you have been taught to do so. Never use equipment unless a **qualified coach** is present.

Warming up

All gymnasts warm up before training to avoid strains and other injuries. It is important to **mobilise** the joints and stretch the muscles before attempting movements.

Stretches

The warm-up session should begin with at least three minutes of a **pulse**-raising activity, which will increase your body temperature. After this you should do some stretches to help your **suppleness**.

⟵ This exercise mobilises your ankles and wrists. Sit down with your feet out in front of you. Extend your ankles one at a time while making 'wave' motions with your hands.

Straddle position ⟶

Sit with your legs extended out sideways. Stretch out with your arms to reach your toes. This stretches your sides, lower back, hips and legs.

⟵ Pike fold

The pike fold is very good for stretching the hamstring muscles in the backs of your thighs. Try to get your chest down to your thighs without bending your knees.

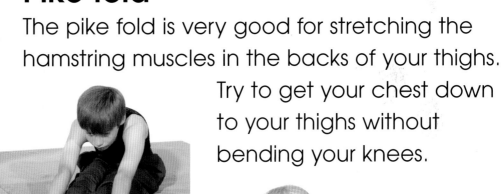

Cobra stretch ⟶

Gymnasts use this exercise to help mobilise the spine. It must be done carefully and slowly.

Relaxing

After doing exercises that really change the natural shape of the spine, it is a good idea to curl up into a ball for a few seconds. This will help return everything to normal.

Posture, strength and flexibility

Gymnasts need to have the right posture when they do their activities. This means standing up straight with the head, shoulders, hips and feet all in line.

Gymnasts must also improve their strength and flexibility. Being strong and flexible will help them learn new skills.

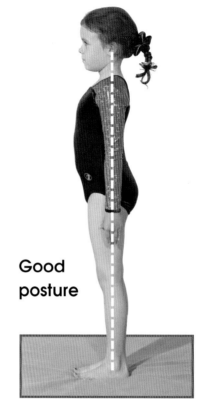

Good posture

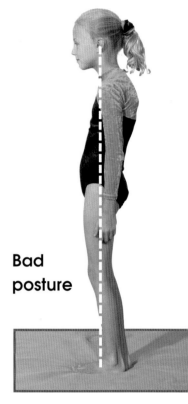

Bad posture

Press ups

Lie down with your hands flat on the floor near your shoulders. Push up with your arms and raise your chest off the floor. Then bend your arms so your chin and chest lower to the floor. Don't let your forehead touch the floor. Try to repeat this exercise ten times.

Sit ups

Lie back with your legs bent and feet flat on the floor. Cross your hands over your chest. Use your tummy muscles to pull yourself up to a sitting position, then lower your shoulders back to the ground slowly. Try to do this ten times.

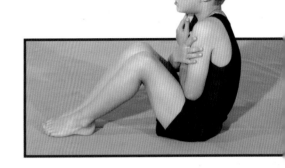

Side splits

Gymnasts who have good flexibility can do the splits. You will have to practise hard before you can do them properly.

Bridge

Lie on your back with your hands on the floor by your head and your fingertips pointing towards your feet. Push your hips and stomach upwards and straighten your arms. Your shoulders should be over your hands. You may need help to get into this position.

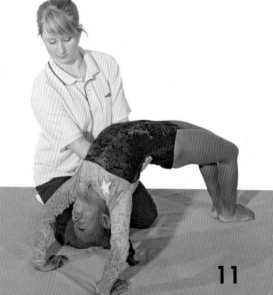

Shapes

The shapes or positions that a gymnast makes with their body are the basis of gymnastics and used at all levels. It is important to learn how to make the shapes and then be able to move easily from one shape to another.

The straight shape

The straight shape is one of the most important shapes in gymnastics. It is often used in the handstand position. You have to be very strong in the middle and flexible in the shoulders to make and hold this shape properly.

The pike, tuck, star and straddle shapes

These shapes can be made while you are still or in the air when you jump. You can also use them as interesting entries and exits from basic skills. Try to copy what these gymnasts (right) are doing.

The pike

Front and back support

To do the front support, put your hands shoulder-width apart with your fingers spread and pointing forwards. Your body should be in a straight line from your shoulders to your feet.

For a back support do the same but start on your back. Push your hips upwards and pull in your tummy and bottom so your body is in a straight line. Make sure your fingers are pointing towards your feet.

The star

The tuck

The straddle

Balances

A balance is a shape that is made and held. You need very good control of your body to keep a still balance. When you have got into the balance position, try to hold it for three seconds without wobbling. Then gently come out of the balance.

Shoulder stand →

Lie on the floor with your hands beside you. Push down against the floor with your arms and bring your knees into your chest, then raise your legs. Raise your body and legs into a **vertical** position.

← V-sit

Start by sitting on the floor in a pike shape. Then raise your legs up so you are balanced on your bottom making a V-shape. Use your arms for **stability** and style.

14

Straddle hold →

This position requires a lot of strength and balance. Start by sitting on the floor in the straddle position. Put your hands flat on the floor in front of you. Press down on the floor and lift your bottom and legs up.

← Arabesque

While standing on one leg lift the other leg straight out behind you. Try to bring your back leg up as high as possible. Use your arms for balance.

Y–stand →

This is a difficult position to do. You need good flexibility and balance. Stand on one leg and lift the other leg upwards and sideways. Use your hand to help lift and hold your leg in position. See if you can get both legs straight without falling over.

Basic floor skills

Once you have learned some shapes and balances, you will want to learn some moves to link them with. **Rotational** skills, such as the forward roll and backward roll are often used to link shapes in floor **sequences**.

Backward roll

A backward roll (below) can be difficult to learn so most beginners start off using a slope to help them.

Forward roll

1. Start the forward roll with your head up, arms outstretched in front of you and balanced in the squat position on the balls of your feet.

Backward roll

1. Stand up straight at the top of a slope. Sit into a tuck shape then topple backwards rolling onto your back.

Warning!
A qualified coach should be present and watching you when you first learn these moves.

2. Place your hands on the floor, tuck your head in and push with your feet, rolling forward onto your shoulders.

3. If you push hard with your feet you will gain enough **momentum** to propel you into a standing finishing position.

2. Put your hands down by your ears and push down hard. Your legs and bottom will carry on over your head and you will land on your feet.

3. Once your feet touch the floor, straighten your knees and stand up.

Advanced floor skills

Headstands

Put your hands on the floor about shoulder-width apart. Then put your head on the ground so that your head and hands form a triangle. Lift your hips up until your back is straight. Then gently lift your feet off the floor and move your knees into the tuck position. When you can do this easily, you can try and straighten your legs.

Handstands

Handstands are one of the most useful skills in gymnastics.

Handstands

1. Start by standing with good posture.

2. Take a big step forward and bend your front knee.

3. Reach down to the floor with straight arms and fingers spread and swing your legs up one at a time.

Try to keep your body in as straight a line as possible.

Cartwheels

Cartwheels are great fun to perform. When learning to do a cartwheel use a semi-circle shape on the floor to show you where to put your hands and legs. Try to put your hands and feet down one at a time (step, hand, hand, foot, foot).

The perfect cartwheel

As you get better you should travel in a straight line and your body should turn in a complete circle – you won't need to use any shapes on the floor to do a perfect cartwheel.

Jumping

Most apparatus activities involve jumping and leaping. It is very important to learn how to jump and land properly.

How to jump

Stand with good posture, then bend your knees and swing your arms downwards. Press hard on the floor with your feet, straighten your legs and swing your arms upwards. Make sure your body, arms and legs are straight and stretched during the jump. When you land, the balls of your feet should touch the ground first, then your heels. Your knees should bend to soften the landing.

This picture shows the three stages of a jump.

Jump or leap
The difference between a jump and a leap is that with a jump you take off and land on two feet. For a leap you take off with one foot and land on the other.

Leaps

A gymnast must spring from one foot and land on the other. It is important to leap high and gracefully.

One of the first leaps you could learn is the split leap (right). Use a run-up to get up some speed, take off from one foot, and stretch your other foot upwards and forwards. Land on the stretched foot and continue to travel forwards.

Stag leap

1. Start as you would for a split leap. Keep one leg bent as you take off.

2. Your front leg should stay bent in this position as you are in the air.

3. Stretch your front leg out for landing. Try to land as neatly as you can.

The beam and vault

When you have learned the basic shapes, balances and moves you can try working on pieces of apparatus.

The beam

Most of the skills you learn on the floor can be performed on the beam. The beam is only 10cm wide so your balance has to be really good. Start on a low beam so you needn't worry about falling off. First practise walking along the beam. You need to concentrate on your posture and looking ahead.

When you have become more confident, you can start to balance on one leg and do positions like the arabesque. Later you can move onto leaps, jumps, rolls and handstands.

The vault

All gymnasts use a springboard for vaulting. It gives them lots of height and bounce onto the vault.

Run up towards the board, then take off from one foot and land on the top of the springboard with two feet. If you jump hard enough you will bounce high into the air. Lift your arms up high and land on both feet.

To do a straddle vault you have to bounce from the springboard then put your hands on the top of the vault. Lift your hips and stretch your legs wide apart to clear the vault. Bring your legs back together to land with your feet together on the other side.

Bars

Parallel bars

The **parallel** bar movements include a wide variety of hangs, swings and balances and require good strength.

In the straight-arm support your arms must be straight and your body rigid. You must press your shoulders down away from your ears, hold your chin up and look straight ahead.

The straight-arm support

This is called the upper-arm support. The body is supported on the upper arms.

This is the hang support or Russian hang. The body hangs from the arms and the legs are pulled over so they are parallel with the bars.

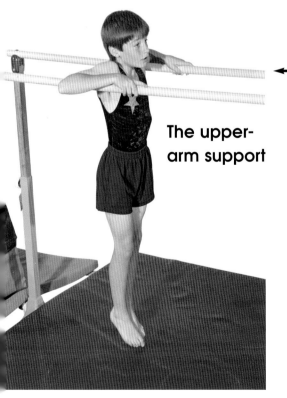

The upper-arm support

The Russian hang

Asymmetric bars

The **asymmetric** bars consist of two bars at different heights. A routine on the asymmetric bars includes swings, circles, handstand positions and many catches and releases.

Most gymnasts use chalk to stop their hands from slipping off the bars.

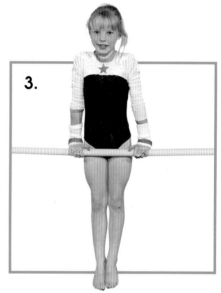

These pictures above show the sequence of the chin circle. This skill is used for getting onto the bars.

1. First you have to do a chin up. Pull hard and bend your arms so you lift yourself off the floor. **2.** Then lift your legs up and pull your hips towards the bar, so you begin to circle around backwards. **3.** Finally lift your body up to front support and point your feet down to the floor so you are 'perched' on the bar.

Floor routine

The floor event gives gymnasts the chance to really show off what they can do!

A floor routine lasts between 70-90 seconds. It must include **elements** that move forwards and backwards and elements that demonstrate strength, balance and flexibility, as well as including leaps and jumps. It must also show changes of speed and level.

These are some of the moves that might be included in a floor routine.

2. She performs a cartwheel and then a forward roll.

1. The gymnast begins in a posed starting position.

Competitions

In a competition, a gymnast must perform on each piece of apparatus. A panel of judges scores each routine. There is no maximum score. The gymnast has to use the most difficult skills and connections to score as many points as possible.

3. Then she does a backward **walkover**.

4. She ends the routine in the splits position.

Glossary

apparatus the equipment used in a gym

asymmetric being different in size, shape or position

element an individual gymnastic skill

flexibility the ability to move around and bend easily

leotard a stretchy, tight-fitting outfit used for dance or exercise

mobilise to make something moveable

momentum the energy and speed in a movement

parallel being side by side and the same distance apart

pulse the rhythm of the heartbeat

qualified coach someone who has been trained so they can teach the sport

rotational something that moves around in a circular way

sequence doing things in a particular order

stability being able to stand still without moving

suppleness the ability to move easily and gracefully

vertical something that is upright

walkover a move where a gymnast turns a complete circle from feet to hands to feet again. A walkover can be done forwards or backwards.

Further reading

The Gymnastics Book: The Young Performer's Guide to Gymnastics, Elfi Schlegel and Claire Ross Dunn, Firefly Books, 2007

I Love Gymnastics, Naia Bray-Moffatt, Dorling Kindersley, 2005

My Best Book of Gymnastics, Christine Morley, Kingfisher Books Ltd, 2003

Gymnastics: Superguides, Joan Jackman, Dorling Kindersley, 2000

Further information

It is easy to get started in gymnastics. To find out more you can contact your local leisure centre, a registered club or British Gymnastics.

British Gymnastics
Ford Hall
Lilleshall National Sports Centre
Newport
Shropshire
TF10 9NB
Tel: 0845 1297129
Email: information@british-gymnastics.org
Website: www.british-gymnastics.org

Gymnastics Australia
607 Canterbury Road
Surrey Hills
VIC 3127
Email: ausgym@gymnastics.org.au
Website: www.gymnastics.org.au

Index